SOUNDS LiKE READING™
BOOK FIVE

The Thing on the Wing Can Sing

A SHORT VOWEL SOUNDS BOOK WITH CONSONANT DIGRAPHS

Brian P. Cleary

illustrations by
Jason Miskimins

Consultant:
Alice M. Maday

Ph.D. in Early Childhood Education with a Focus in Literacy
Assistant Professor, Retired
Department of Curriculum and Instruction
University of Minnesota

M Millbrook Press/Minneapolis

to Mrs. Somlai, my fourth-grade teacher in
Richfield, Minnesota, and to Mrs. Simoneau, my
(second) fourth-grade teacher in Rocky River, Ohio
—B.P.C.

Text copyright © 2009 by Brian P. Cleary
Illustrations copyright © 2009 by Lerner Publishing Group, Inc.

Millbrook Press
A division of Lerner Publishing Group, Inc.
241 First Avenue North
Minneapolis, MN 55401 U.S.A.

Website address: www.lernerbooks.com

Library of Congress Cataloging-in-Publication Data

Cleary, Brian P., 1959–
    The thing on the wing can sing : a short vowel sounds book with consonant
 digraphs / by Brian P. Cleary ; illustrations by Jason Miskimins ;
 consultant: Alice M. Maday.
      p.   cm. — (Sounds like reading)
   ISBN: 978-0-8225-7639-6 (lib. bdg. : alk. paper)
   1. English language—Vowels—Juvenile literature. 2. English language—
Consonants—Juvenile literature. 3. English language—Phonetics—Juvenile
literature. 4. Reading—Phonetic method—Juvenile literature. I. Miskimins,
Jason, ill. II. Maday, Alice M. III. Title.
 PE1157.C57 2009
 428.1'3—dc22   2008012771

Manufactured in the United States of America
1 2 3 4 5 6 – BP – 14 13 12 11 10 09

Dear Parents and Educators,

As a former adult literacy coach and the father of three children, I know that learning to read isn't always easy. That's why I developed **Sounds Like Reading**™—a series that uses a combination of devices to help children learn to read.

This book is the fifth in the **Sounds Like Reading**™ series. It uses rhyme, repetition, illustration, and phonics to introduce young readers to short vowel sounds and consonant digraphs—letter combinations that come together to create a new sound. These include combinations such as *ch*, *sh*, and *th*. I've chosen to use a broad, inclusive definition of digraphs in this book, so you'll also see combinations such as *kn*, *ng*, and *ck*.

Starting on page 4, you'll see three rhyming words on each left-hand page. These words are part of the sentence on the facing page. They all feature short vowels and consonant digraphs. As the book progresses, the sentences become more challenging. These sentences contain a "discovery" word—an extra rhyming word in addition to those that appear on the left. Toward the end of the book, the sentences contain two discovery words. Children will delight in the increased confidence that finding and decoding these words will bring. They'll also enjoy looking for the mouse that appears throughout the book. The mouse asks readers to look for words that sound alike.

The bridge to literacy is one of the most important we will ever cross. It is my hope that the **Sounds Like Reading**™ series will help young readers to hop, gallop, and skip from one side to the other!

Sincerely,

Brian P. Cleary
Brian P. Cleary

Look for me to help you find the words that sound alike!

chin

shin

thin

Can you find three words that sound alike?

4

His **chin** and his **shin** are **thin**.

knock

rock

clock

Knock on the **rock** by the **clock**.

thing

wing

sing

The **thing** on the **wing** can **sing**.

trash

sash

Miss Beauty Queen

ash

Miss Beauty Quee

The **trash** by the **sash** was filled with **ash**.

witch

ditch

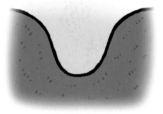

itch

The **witch** in the **ditch** began to **itch**.

long

song

wrong

The **long song** was all **wrong**.

batch

patch

latch

Can you find the word that sounds like batch, patch, and latch?

16

Snatch the **batch** from the **patch** by the **latch**.

tack

black

rack

Can you find the word that sounds like tack, black, and rack?

The **tack** is **back** on the **black rack**.

duck

stuck

muck

Chuck and the **duck** are **stuck** in the **muck**.

speck

wreck

deck

Can you find the word that sounds like speck, wreck, and deck?

Check the **speck** by the **wreck** on the **deck**.

whip

chip

ship

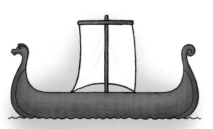

Can you find the word that sounds like whip, chip, and ship?

A **whip** and a **chip** are at the **tip** of the **ship**.

snack

sack

stack

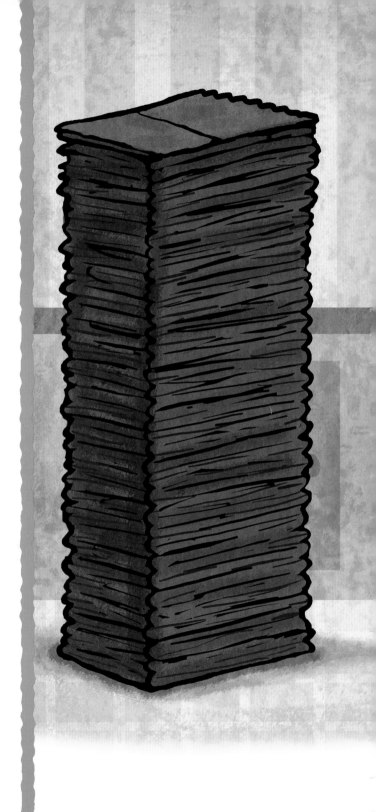

Pack the **snack** in a **sack** from the **stack.**

bunch

munch

punch

Can you find two words that sound like bunch, munch, and punch?

The **bunch** has a **hunch** that they will **munch** and drink **punch** at **lunch**.

Brian P. Cleary is the author of the best-selling Words Are CATegorical® series as well as the Math Is CATegorical® and Adventures in Memory™ series. He has also written several picture books and poetry books. In addition to his work as a children's author and humorist, Mr. Cleary has been a tutor in an adult literacy program. He lives in Cleveland, Ohio.

Jason Miskimins grew up in Cincinnati, Ohio, and graduated from the Columbus College of Art & Design in 2003. He currently lives in North Olmsted, Ohio, where he works as an illustrator of books and greeting cards.

Alice M. Maday has a master's degree in early childhood education from Butler University in Indianapolis, Indiana, and a Ph.D. in early childhood education, with a focus in literacy, from the University of Minnesota in Minneapolis. Dr. Maday has taught at the college level as well as in elementary schools and preschools throughout the country. In addition, she has served as an emergent literacy educator for kindergarten and first-grade students in Germany for the U.S. Department of Defense. Her research interests include the kindergarten curriculum, emergent literacy, parent and teacher expectations, and the place of preschool in the reading readiness process.

For even more phonics fun, check out all eight SOUNDS LiKE READING™ titles listed on the back of this book!

And find activities, games, and more at www.brianpcleary.com.